Ring of Confidence

Penny Vine and Teresa Todd
Foreword by Jenny Mosley

Positive Press

FIRST PUBLISHED 2001 BY LEEDS CITY COUNCIL
IN ASSOCIATION WITH POSITIVE PRESS LTD

Reissued with new cover 2003
Positive Press Ltd
28a Gloucester Road
Trowbridge
Wiltshire
BA14 0AA

Text © Penny Vine & Teresa Todd

ISBN 0-9540585-1-8

Printed by:

HERON PRESS
19-24 White Hays North,
West Wilts Trading Estate,
Westbury,
Wiltshire BA13 4JT.

contents

Foreword

This is a much needed book. Many early years practitioners will greet this book with a long sigh of relief! We are in a climate of recommendations where we are being urged to help children to become 'safe' against the dangers around them. The tension for teachers is how to achieve the aim of helping children become emotionally and physically safe, whilst at the same time safeguarding their right to innocence and a childhood untroubled by adult concerns.

Some early years practitioners lack the confidence to take difficult scenarios and troubling facts into the safe, colourful 'worlds of discovery' they have created in their nurseries and classrooms. Yet all the research and endless everyday news constantly reminds us how our children are vulnerable to a range of personal and social dangers. We need to find a way we can help them explore these issues that is in harmony with our child-centred teaching styles and commitment to play and self discovery.

This book will help many teachers find just the 'way in' they were looking for. Penny and Teresa use the 'five steps to empowerment' of Quality Circle Time to underpin the lesson structures; thereby keeping the lessons lively, yet emotionally safe. These 'steps' were constructed by me initially to help children relax and practice the skills of self-expression whilst leading into the 'opening-up' of more difficult and challenging issues, then moving away from this activity towards more celebratory, fun and playful circle games.

Using their own unique creativity, sensitivity, and imagination, Penny and Teresa have created a rich 'weave' of games, puppet activities and relaxation strategies to help children explore potentially worrying scenarios which alert them to all the dangers and ways to survive; yet leaves them feeling untroubled by the experience and personally stronger and more capable. For young children the circle time approach, if handled by trained, sensitive teachers, is an extraordinarily

'safe' vehicle. It is so naturally a part of their everyday life that its rituals soothe and protect children from any sense of 'alarm'. The puppets too, are a part of their everyday emotional life, and it is only natural the puppets will seek the advice of the children. By giving advice the children are learning that they have answers inside them – that they are agents of change, that they are not passive victims. By drawing upon their own inner resources in order to help their friends, the puppets, out of sadness or danger, they are only a short developmental step away from soon being able to help themselves and others out of similar dangers. Because their ideas and suggestions are rewarded by the puppets thanking them and sounding happier, the children learn that they 'make a difference', happy endings can happen when everyone works together.

Self-esteem is built when key people in your life reflect back to you that you are valuable, worthy of respect and that your ideas matter. The puppets, handled by their own important teacher, reflect back to children that they too are wise, worthy of being listened to. If you feel good about yourself you will make sounder choices to protect yourself from future harm. But children also learn that talking about things makes things better. By the act of talking regularly with each other and the puppets they are learning that talking can release feelings, let light into darkness, draw good people to you, helps you make wise decisions, create friendships and gets you help!

This is an essential book for all early years practitioners concerned to help 'their' children become confident, insightful and emotionally intelligent citizens for the future!

Jenny Mosley

Director of the Whole School Quality Circle Time Model

Ring of Confidence
Practitioners' comments

This pack makes an important contribution to the Early Years Personal, Social and Emotional curriculum. As a practitioner, I welcome this well thought out and clearly presented programme. It combines the Quality Circle Time structure and ethos with excellent Health Education and Personal Safety principles and practice. "Ring of Confidence" should give practitioners the confidence to support children in developing the skills, knowledge and understanding and attitudes we know are of vital importance to them yet sometimes feel unconfident and unskilled in addressing. At the heart of this programme is ensuring that children are supported in feeling and keeping safe and each lesson has been carefully planned with this in mind. Parental involvement, assessment and celebrating children's achievements are addressed thoughtfully. This programme is an invaluable addition to work on empowering young people, developing children's emotional intelligence and their ability to meet the challenges of life - please use it!"

Helen Price, Early Years Practitioner

This resource will make planning for the emotional needs of young children a simpler task, resulting in quality work that begins to raise awareness about safety and substance abuse. Children will love the puppets, games and circle time activities. Practitioners will appreciate the clear format, ideas for assessment and the detailed framework for provision that comes with each unit, linked to the Early Learning Goals.

Claire Bevington, Head Teacher

"Ring Of Confidence" signals an important landmark in encouraging and supporting teachers to tackle what are real and difficult issues for children.

If schools are to take their responsibilities for child protection seriously and address prevention of abuse as well as protection and support, they need to offer opportunities for all children to acquire the appropriate skills, knowledge and understanding and attitudes. This material provides a clear comprehensive and developmental programme integrated within existing structures for personal social and emotional education.

I am particularly pleased to see this important area given the same rigorous monitoring, recording and evaluation which is required of other subjects.

Mary Armitage, Child Protection Officer, Education Leeds

Acknowledgments

We would like to thank the following
people for their support
in the development of this document:

**Sally Threlfall – Coordinator of the
Early Excellence Centre Network, Seacroft**

Sylvia Lunn – Standards Officer, Education Leeds

Maureen Hochstrasser – Nursery Teacher, Brudenell Primary School

Thanks also to the following people for their support
in the production of this document:

**Debbie Axup and Darren West from
'The Front Room' Design Bureau**

Finally, a huge thank you to
Jenny Mosley for her continuing inspiration!

Ring of Confidence Introduction

No setting can achieve excellence without first attending to the personal, social and emotional development of its children. Children need to feel safe if they are to achieve their full potential. A nurturing environment where children experience emotional well being can support children in becoming competent in looking after themselves and coping with every day living. An effective Personal, Social, Health and Citizenship Education programme can help children deal with risk and help them to meet the challenges of life, now and in the future. Personal, Social, Health and Citizenship Education can assist children in developing positive self-esteem and confidence so that they can take increasing control of and responsibility for their lives.

This publication aims to promote children's welfare, safety and emotional well being. It is concerned with two aspects of safety:

- Personal Safety and Use of Substances

The two aspects were chosen in light of three key documents:

- Curriculum Guidance Document for the Foundation Stage 2000
- Working Together To Safeguard Children [Department of Health] 1999
- Tackling Drugs To Build A Better Britain [The Government's 10 Year Strategy For Tackling Drug Misuse] 1998

All the documents stress the importance of enabling children to acquire – both in and out of formal education settings – the skills needed to:

- Develop self awareness, positive self-esteem and confidence
- Stay as healthy as possible
- Keep themselves safe
- Have worthwhile and fulfilling relationships
- Respect the differences between people
- Develop independence and responsibility
- Play an active role as members of a democratic society
- Make the most of their own and others' abilities

Building an emotionally & physically safe environment

Through their day-to-day contact with children and families, practitioners have a key role in maintaining a safe environment for children. They support children in understanding what is and is not acceptable behaviour towards them. They help children to develop skills in staying safe and encourage children to speak up if they have worries and concerns. Emotional safety is at the heart of Quality Circle Time and is modelled through the practitioner's verbal and non-verbal behaviours. Groundrules ensure that children know that listening to each other and treating others with respect, care and concern are the foundation of supportive relationships.

Throughout the lesson plans games are played that teach children valuable skills in relationship building. Many of the games intentionally involve touch. Touch can be both a source of immense comfort and sadly, part of abusive relationships. It is our experience that many children need appropriate touch 'modelling' for them. They need to learn how to ask for permission before touching each other. This can be extremely hard for young children so we are recommending that you teach children the following hand symbol.

 Thumb Up
Okay to touch

 Thumb Down
Not okay to touch

This symbol will appear at the top of each game and ending ritual as a reminder to the practitioner that the hand symbol needs rehearsing before you play the game or do the ending ritual.

We believe that teaching the hand symbol will have a major impact on decreasing abusive behaviours. We strongly recommend that this approach be integrated into your child protection procedures. We also suggest that parents are involved in this work and the hand symbol explained to them. It is our experience that when fully involved, most parents support and can endorse key messages of safety.

Lesson 5 and lesson 6 in the Personal Safety section deals with the sensitive issue of OK and not OK touches, safe and unsafe secrets. We recommend that practitioners involve their Child Protection Officer before carrying out the lessons. Involvement of parents is crucial throughout the programme but especially for lessons 5 and 6. It is our experience that when fully involved, most parents support and can endorse key messages of safety.

Paying attention to the learning environment can further enhance Quality Circle Time. You can do this by:

● Having music playing as children settle themselves

● Having beanbags or chairs for the children to sit on

● Welcoming each child with a phrase and a smile

● Lighting a candle to start and end Quality Circle Time

Building an emotionally & physically safe environment

Our publication is divided into two sections. Each section consists of:

- Medium term planning
- Lesson plans
- Additional resource sheets.

We hope this publication will support children in moving safely, responsibly and courageously in the personal and social worlds they inhabit. Worlds where the ability to understand their emotions, to be able to listen to others, to empathize and to express emotions appropriately are as much of a passport to opportunity as academic qualifications.

The lessons in the publication use the Quality Circle Time model as advocated by Jenny Mosley which is developed, structured and thoughtful, and has the needs of the learning child firmly at the centre of its pedagogy. Quality Circle Time is a process based approach to learning which aims to enhance emotional well being, encouraging self awareness, empathy and positive communication. Participants not familiar with Quality Circle Time are advised to read 'Quality Circle Time In The Primary Classroom' - J. Mosley, 'Here We Go Round' J. Mosley and H. Sonnet.

Definition of Terms

Throughout this publication we use the term setting to mean local authority nurseries, nursery centres, playgroups, pre-schools, accredited childminders in approved childminding networks, or schools in the independent, private or voluntary sectors, and maintained schools.

The adults who work with the children in the settings, whatever their qualifications, are referred to as **practitioners.**

The word **parents** is used to refer to mothers, fathers, legal guardians and the primary carers of children in public care.

The term **curriculum** is used to describe everything children do, see, hear or feel in their setting, both planned and unplanned.

Assessment

Assessment within this framework is in keeping with the principles of the Curriculum Guidance for the Foundation Stage (QCA September 2000). Effective assessment involves systematic observation, sensitive interaction and talking and listening to children. Assessment is a key teaching strategy within the foundation stage and should be used to inform planning for the next steps in children's learning.

It is envisaged that the Quality Circle Time sessions are delivered as an integral part of the curriculum and would be one method of planning for the development of the Personal, Social, Citizenship, Health and Emotional needs of the children. The suggestions within the medium term plans for other activities are intended to provide an ongoing context for revisiting the learning objectives in meaningful and relevant ways, thus helping children to consolidate their learning. They also give opportunities for children to express and demonstrate their developing skills, knowledge and attitudes in those areas explored during Quality Circle Time. Observation of children during their independent and adult supported work and play will give opportunities for assessment. It is important

that these observations are made in the normal context of the setting in order to assess whether children are using them in their everyday work and play. They will be ongoing throughout the time that the work is being undertaken but assessment towards the end of the work/unit is important.

It is also important to involve parents in the assessment process. You can inform them about the content of the Quality Circle Time sessions and topic via newsletters, notice boards and direct contact. Talk to them about what they notice their child is doing and talking about at home. Record this in the child's profile or record or if possible get parents to do this themselves.

Assessment Opportunities

LEARN HOW TO KEEP THEMSELVES AND OTHERS SAFE (PERSONAL)		
Lesson	**Assessment**	**Possible Contexts**
One	The child is beginning to use the language of feelings The child is able to say what makes them sad, happy, angry and frightened	Role-play In small group activity or one–one as situations arise
Two	The child can indicate who they would turn to if they had a worry	Mark making area Book corner talking about a book
Three	The child can identify what makes them feel safe or unsafe	Show either through drawing, pictures or orally
Four	The children can talk about safety rules	Draw or talk about in small group or in role play
Five	The child can identify what makes them feel not OK	Draw a picture or talk in small group or in role of play
Six	The child can talk about a safe and an unsafe secret	In role play area

LEARN HOW TO KEEP THEMSELVES AND OTHERS SAFE (SUBSTANCE)		
Lesson	**Assessment**	**Possible Contexts**
One	The child is able to sort objects into those that are safe to put **onto** their body and those that are not safe to put **onto** their body	Interactive display Talking in small groups
Two	The child is able to sort objects/pictures into those that are safe to put **into** its body and those that are not safe to put **into** its body	Interactive display Talking in small groups
Three	The child can talk about what Teddy feels like when he is not well The child can suggest ways to help Teddy feel better	Role play area Small world props
Four	The child can tell or draw simple safety rules The child is beginning to explain why such rules are necessary	Mark making
Five	The child can sort photographs into safe and not safe sets The child is comfortable with asking for help	Interactive display Give the children photographs of things that are safe to play with and things that are not

Medium Term Planning
Unit 1

Theme
KEEPING MYSELF SAFE

Expected Duration
(to be completed by practitioner)

FOCUS
Keeping Myself Safe **KEY AREAS OF LEARNING** Personal Social and Emotional Development, Communication, Language and Literacy

Children will have opportunities to learn:

SKILLS

Able to identify and recognise a range of feelings and emotions in themselves and others

Able to identify those who listen to us and those we can trust

Able to tell when they feel safe or unsafe

Able to differentiate between OK and not OK touches

Able to differentiate between safe or an unsafe secret

Able to listen, negotiate, make simple choices and assert themselves

ATTITUDES

Value themselves and others

Value emotions as an aid to thinking

Develop respect for self and others

Appreciate the need to take care

Care about keeping themselves and others safe

KNOWLEDGE & CONCEPTS

Know that there are a variety of different people who can help to keep them safe

Know what trust means

Know that they have rights over their own bodies

Know that different places have different rules

Know about how people are feeling and how I am feeling

Know their own name, address and telephone number

FOCUSED ACTIVITIES AND EXPERIENCES:	Early Learning Goals
Invite visitors, e.g. local police officer, dinner-supervisor, lollipop person, security officer from supermarket to visit the setting, to talk about how they can help the children to keep safe.	CLL8
Talk about the rules for the setting. Using pictures/photos talk about rules for other places they go to, e.g. their place of worship, in the street, in the supermarket, on the bus.	PSE7
Draw up some rules for keeping safe, display them, share them with parents and carers	PSE8
Using photos/pictures from magazines talk about what is happening and what people might be feeling. Help children to 'read' the facial expressions and body language.	PSE4
Using feelings faces talk with children about when they have felt different feelings.	PSE3
Play trust games, e.g. blindfolded children are helped around an obstacle course by a friend.	PSE7
Set up role play of the house of the Three Bears or Little Red Riding Hood	CLL17
Introduce scenario into role- play for children to problem solve, e.g. a letter from daddy Bear to Goldilocks' mummy, explaining what had happened at their house. What will mummy do?	CLL16
Write letter back (group/individual)	CLL12

INVOLVEMENT OF PARENTS

Newsletter to parents: 'We are learning about keeping ourselves safe' and ways they can reinforce this at home

Ask parents to help children learn and remember their name, address and telephone number

Invitation to assembly about 'Keeping Safe'

ENHANCEMENTS OF BASIC PROVISION AND INTERACTIVE DISPLAYS

Question of the day 'How do you feel today?' Respond to feelings faces

Small world/small construction 'people who help us set' Lego Zoo/park

Role Play: Props for Goldilocks and Three Bears, Little Red Riding Hood

Story props for above stories

RESOURCES: EQUIPMENT, MATERIALS, PICTURES

Feeling faces

Mirrors for children

Puppets/props to retell stories

Role play props for people who help us for use outside

RESOURCES: BOOKS, POEMS, SONGS, RHYMES

Goldilocks and the Three Bears, Little Red Riding Hood

'If you're happy and you know it'

VOCABULARY

Glad, happy, sad, angry, cross, frightened, proud, kind/unkind, like/don't like

Rules, OK secrets/not OK secrets, safe/unsafe, tell, listen, left out,

Parent, carer, adult, police, trust, bully,

Real, pretend

QUESTIONS (PRESENT, FUTURE, PAST)

What did you do when...?

How did you feel when...?

What would you do if...?

I wonder how you might feel if...?

I wonder how he/she feels...?

OBSERVATIONAL ASSESSMENT OPPORTUNITIES

Observe children's use of the language of feelings in their role play

(Please refer to Assessment Section included in lesson plans)

Evaluation

What went well?

What would I change next time?

Feedback from Children

Feedback from parents

Quality Circle Time Rules

We listen to each other

We do not say or do anything that would hurt another person

We signal when we want to say something

Learn to keep themselves and others safe

Foundation Lesson 1

I am going to learn about how I can move safely and confidently in the world I know

1. THE MAIN AREA OF STUDY SUGGESTS THAT PUPILS SHOULD:	2. KEY LEARNING OBJECTIVES
SKILLS ● Be able to identify and recognise a range of feelings and emotions in themselves and others	● I can tell you what makes me feel angry, sad, happy, frightened
ATTITUDES ● Value emotions as an aid to thinking	● I 'listen' to my feelings Practitioner needs to model this attitude for the children.
KNOWLEDGE/UNDERSTANDING ● Know about how people are feeling and how I am feeling	● I use all my skills, particularly my looking and listening skills to tell how people are feeling

3. GROUND RULES	4. SKILLS AWARENESS
● We listen to each other ● We do not say or do anything that would hurt another person ● We signal when we want to say something	● Concentrating ● Listening ● Looking ● Speaking ● Thinking Throughout Quality Circle Time it is vital that practitioners praise children for using the above skills

5. GAME 1

FIND YOUR FEELING FACE

- Collect a selection of music suggesting different emotions

- Each child is given a feeling face card, which they do not look at

- The music begins

- Children walk around the room and when the music stops they look at their card and mimic the face on the card

- They find the other children who have the same face as them

6. ROUND 1

Pass the plastic mirror around the circle and ask children to say how they are feeling today

Trigger sentence:

I am feeling...

7. SILENT STATEMENTS

Stand up and cross the circle if:

You are wearing blue

You are wearing red

You are wearing trousers

You feel happy sitting on your own reading a book

You feel sad when your parent leaves you at nursery/school

You feel frightened when you think you are lost

You feel angry when someone hurts you

8. OPEN FORUM

The practitioner tells the children that she has just seen puppet in the cloakroom. He had his head in hands (practitioner models) crying quietly. When practitioner asked him what was wrong puppet didn't say anything.

Practitioner: I wonder what puppet is feeling?

Children respond

Practitioner: I wonder what we should do?

Children respond

The practitioner values all the children's responses. She brings puppet into the classroom.

Puppet: I'm feeling really sad today, can you guess why?

Children respond

Puppet: the other puppets wouldn't let me play with the blocks and I really like my friends and I get sad when they won't let me play. What can I do?

Children respond

9. GAME 2	10. ENDING RITUAL
FIND YOUR FEELING FACE ● Collect a selection of music suggesting different emotions ● Each child is given a feeling face card, which they do not look at ● The music begins ● Children walk around the room and when the music stops they look at their card and mimic the face on the card ● They find the other children who have the same face as them	**Pass the smile** The practitioner begins by smiling at the child on the left of her When the child on the left has been smiled at they repeat by smiling at the child on their left

11. ASSESSMENT	12. RESOURCES
The child is able to say what makes them sad, happy, angry and frightened	● Activity Sheet 1 - Feeling faces ● Puppet

Learn to keep themselves and others safe

Foundation Lesson 2

I am going to learn about different people who can help to make me safe

1. THE MAIN AREA OF STUDY SUGGESTS THAT PUPILS SHOULD:	2. KEY LEARNING OBJECTIVES
SKILLS ● Able to identify those who listen to us and those we can trust	● I can tell you who listens to me
ATTITUDES ● Value themselves and others	● I show through my actions, my words and the way I treat others, that I value my peer group and myself
KNOWLEDGE/UNDERSTANDING ● Know what trust means ● Know that there area variety of different people who can help to keep them safe	● I know what trust means. I can tell you some of the people that I can turn to when I need help

3. GROUND RULES	4. SKILLS AWARENESS
● We listen to each other ● We do not say or do anything that would hurt another person ● We signal when we want to say something	● Concentrating ● Listening ● Looking ● Speaking ● Thinking Throughout Quality Circle Time it is vital that practitioners praise children for using the above skills

5. GAME 1

- In a circle the practitioner whispers 'duck ', 'cow' or 'cat' to each child

- Children move around the group making 'quack', 'moo', or 'meow' sounds until they are in three groups

- You can give children animal picture cards to support them

6. ROUND 1

Puppet talks to the children about a nasty dream that she had had last night. In the dream:

She lost her mummy at the shops and didn't know what to do. The dream has scared her. Can the children help her? If the children had a problem whom could they go to?

If I have a problem...

Trigger sentence:

I could go to …

7. SILENT STATEMENTS

Stand up and cross the circle if:

You are wearing yellow

You are wearing black

You are wearing a skirt

You would go to your practitioner if you feel worried

You would talk to someone at home if someone was hurting you

You would post an unhappy face to tell your practitioner you felt unhappy

8. OPEN FORUM

The puppet tells the children that she has got a problem and she has nobody to talk to.

The practitioner asks the children if they can help the puppet. (Wherever possible use dialogue between the puppet and the children rather than the practitioner and the children).

Children respond

The practitioner reminds the children that they can use their suggestions for themselves when they have a problem.

9. GAME 2

We have chosen a name for the puppet in this game. Obviously you will want to select a name.
Similarly, we have used the term nursery to indicate any foundation stage setting. Please use the term appropriate to your setting.

Selby went to nursery…

When Selby went to nursery yesterday nobody said hello to him. Selby felt ---.

But today everyone waved at him and said ---.

Selby felt ---.

When Selby went to nursery yesterday nobody said do you want to play. Selby felt ---.

But today his friends said---

Selby felt ---

When Selby went to nursery yesterday lots of his friends laughed when Selby hurt his finger.

Selby felt---.

But today, when he hurt his toe, his friends said---

Selby felt---.

When Selby went to school yesterday a bigger puppet took his new ball. All the other puppets didn't do anything.

Selby felt---

But today when the bigger puppet came to take Selby's coat the other puppets---

Selby felt---

(Ensure that children are aware of safety procedures)

10. ENDING RITUAL

Pass the smile

The practitioner begins by smiling at the child on the left of her. When the child on the left has been smiled at they repeat by smiling at the child on their left.

11. ASSESSMENT

Can the children show either through a drawing or orally whom they could turn to if they had a worry?

12. RESOURCES

- Activity Sheet 2 - Animal picture cards

- Puppets

Learn to keep themselves and others safe

Foundation Lesson 3

I am going to learn about 'smiley inside feelings' and 'not smiley inside feelings

1. THE MAIN AREA OF STUDY SUGGESTS THAT PUPILS SHOULD:	2. KEY LEARNING OBJECTIVES
SKILLS ● Able to tell when they feel safe or unsafe	● I can tell what makes me feel safe or unsafe
ATTITUDES ● Care about keeping themselves and others safe	● I am worthy of care and protection
KNOWLEDGE/UNDERSTANDING ● Know how they feel 'inside'	● I am beginning to recognize how I feel 'inside'

3. GROUND RULES	4. SKILLS AWARENESS
● We listen to each other ● We do not say or do anything that would hurt another person ● We signal when we want to say something	● Concentrating ● Listening ● Looking ● Speaking ● Thinking Throughout Quality Circle Time it is vital that practitioners praise children for using the above skills

5. GAME 1

- The children stand in a circle

- The practitioner acts as mirror and the children are the reflections

- The practitioner mimes a series of gentle movements which the children copy

- You could select some gentle music to accompany this activity

6. ROUND 1

The practitioner tells the children that puppet feels scared 'inside'. Can any of the children think what might have happened to puppet to make him feel so scared inside?

A useful way to conceptualise 'inside' for children is to make a visual representation of puppet's heart. The heart has a very scared face on the front.

Children respond

Trigger statement:

Puppet doesn't feel safe when…

7. SILENT STATEMENTS

Stand up and cross the circle if:

You have got a baby in your house

You have got long hair

You like the dark

You don't like loud noises

You feel safe in the toilets

You don't feel safe in the outside area

8. OPEN FORUM

Using one of the children's responses from Round 1, the practitioner asks the children to help puppet solve his problem.

e.g. The children have suggested that puppet feels unsafe inside when big people shout at him.

Practitioner: 'I wonder what puppet could do when big people shout at him?'

Children respond

Puppet: 'That's a good idea. I'm going to have a go at that. Can you say it with me so that I can practise?'

9. GAME 2	10. ENDING RITUAL
Island Rescue	The children pass a back rub around the circle.
● Mats are spread out around the room. Each mat represents an island. Each mat is labelled 1 to 6	The practitioner gently rubs the back of the child to their right. This child then gently rubs the back of the child on their right and so on until the rub has been passed around the circle.
● The children choose one mat to stand on before the game starts. When the music begins the children move around the 'sea'	
● When the music stops the children move quickly to an 'island'	
● The practitioner calls out a number and that 'island' sinks. Ask the children on the safe islands to go and rescue the islanders	
● The game begins again. Eventually all the islands disappear and everyone is together on the last island	

11. ASSESSMENT	12. RESOURCES
Children can draw a picture or say what makes them feel safe or unsafe	● Activity Sheet 3 – Scared Heart
	● Music
	● Numbers 1 to 6
	● Mats
	● Puppet

Learn to keep themselves and others safe

Foundation Lesson 4

I am going to learn how I am going to keep safe when I am away from home

1. THE MAIN AREA OF STUDY SUGGESTS THAT PUPILS SHOULD:	2. KEY LEARNING OBJECTIVES
SKILLS ● Able to tell when they feel safe or unsafe	● I can tell what makes me feel safe or unsafe
ATTITUDES ● Appreciate the need to take care and for safe actions	● I am worthy of care ● I think about the actions I take to care about myself
KNOWLEDGE/UNDERSTANDING ● Know that there are a variety of different people who can help to keep them safe ● Know what keeping safe means	● I know 3 people who can take care of me ● I know some safety rules

3. GROUND RULES	4. SKILLS AWARENESS
● We listen to each other ● We do not say or do anything that would hurt another person ● We signal when we want to say something	● Concentrating ● Listening ● Looking ● Speaking ● Thinking Throughout Quality Circle Time it is vital that practitioners praise children for using the above skills

5. GAME 1

- The children sit in a circle

- The practitioner acts as mirror and the children are the reflections

- The practitioner mimes a series of gentle movements which the children copy

- You could select some gentle music to accompany this activity

6. ROUND 1

Trigger sentence:

'I don't feel safe when...

7. SILENT STATEMENTS

Stand up and cross the circle if:

You have a brother

You live in a flat

You like loud noises

You don't like scary videos/stories

You think puppet is special

The aim of the whole session is to encourage children to value themselves. At this point the practitioner says 'I think puppet is special and I think everybody here is too...' she looks around the circle as she says this making eye contact with every child.

8. OPEN FORUM

A letter arrives for the practitioner from puppet's granddad. The practitioner reads the letter to the children.

The letter tells the practitioner that Grandad is very worried because puppet went out of the garden to play with some big children.

Grandad didn't know where puppet had gone. Could the practitioner have a word with puppet about keeping safe?

The practitioner asks puppet to tell the children what he did last night. Puppet says that he only went to play with some 'friends'.

Practitioner: 'Did you tell Grandad where you were going?'

The dialogue continues with the children offering guidance and support wherever possible.

9. GAME 2	10. ENDING RITUAL
● The children form pairs and sit facing each other cross-legged ● They begin to mirror each other, taking turns to act as the reflection ● The leader chooses a series of simple actions which the 'reflection' copies	We are special The practitioner prepares a special box (with a lift up lid if possible), with a small unbreakable mirror inside. The practitioner tells the children that when they look inside the box they will see someone who is very special. (You can ask the children who they think they will see). The box is passed around the circle and each child opens the box and looks inside. They are not to tell anybody what they have seen until everybody has had a look. When all the children have looked inside the box the practitioner asks the children who they have seen and reaffirms that we are all special

11. ASSESSMENT	12. RESOURCES
Children can talk about safety rules They are beginning to internalize safety rules and demonstrate their understanding in work and play	● Activity Sheet 4 - Letter from Grandad ● Puppet ● Special box with unbreakable mirror inside

Learn to keep themselves and others safe

Foundation Lesson 5

I am going to learn about OK and not OK touches

(before doing this lesson please reread the introduction)

Prior to this Quality Circle Time read *Its My Body* by Lory Freeman, ISBN 0-943990-03-3, obtainable from Smallwood Publishing, Tel: 01304 2269900. The story explores safe touches and teaches young children strategies for resisting uncomfortable touches. We suggest you read the story two or three times to make sure that children are familiar with the key messages. It is also important to involve parents so that they can reinforce and be reassured by the messages you are conveying.

1. THE MAIN AREA OF STUDY SUGGESTS THAT PUPILS SHOULD:	2. KEY LEARNING OBJECTIVES
SKILLS ● Be able to differentiate between OK and not OK touches	● I can tell you what makes me feel OK and what makes me feel not OK
ATTITUDES ● Care about keeping themselves and others safe	● I care about my body
KNOWLEDGE/UNDERSTANDING ● Know that they have rights over their own bodies	● I know that my body belongs to me

3. GROUND RULES	4. SKILLS AWARENESS
● We listen to each other ● We do not say or do anything that would hurt another person ● We signal when we want to say something	● Concentrating ● Listening ● Looking ● Speaking ● Thinking Throughout Quality Circle Time it is vital that practitioners praise children for using the above skills

5. GAME 1

Begin by talking about the different touches we receive and give out

- Ask children to say whether they like hugs, friendly squeezes, handshakes etc. Be sensitive to child protection issues

- A child may like hugs but not from a particular person. Puppet can do a lot of this work for you, e.g. Puppet says: Children, I love hugs from my mummy but I don't like it when my sister tickles me...it's a bit scary...she hugs me too tight as well...

Musical Touch

- Children move around the room to music

- When the music stops they ask the person nearest to them if they can give them a hug

- If a child doesn't want to be hugged suggest a handshake or a friendly smile is exchanged

6. ROUND 1

Discuss comfortable touches and what they may be. How do we feel when we get these touches? Puppet can help by telling the children about her comfortable touches. Stress that we are all different and we may not like the same touches. Ask the children what comfortable touches they like.

Trigger statement:

I like it when...

7. SILENT STATEMENTS

Stand up and cross the circle if:

You are wearing white socks

You have got a pocket in your clothes

You like being cuddled

You don't like being tickled

You like being whirled around

You like having your face stroked

8. OPEN FORUM

Puppet tells the practitioner that he has a problem. The practitioner offers to help.

Puppet: On Mondays Mummy has to go to work, so my sister looks after me. Last Monday we started watching television. The cartoons were on. I love cartoons. My sister started tickling me...I didn't like it...I tried asking her to stop but she wouldn't...she's always doing it and it really upsets me...it makes me scared too and angry! What can I do?

Practitioner reassures puppet and praises puppet for asking for help.

The practitioner asks the children what puppet should do now.

The practitioner role models a positive response to puppet for telling. We know in reality this may not be the case but we have a responsibility to encourage children to tell.

9. GAME 2

- Play 'blue finger'. The practitioner says a colour and a part of the body. Children match up that colour with the part of the body mentioned, e.g. practitioner says, 'blue finger'.

- The children put their finger on something blue that someone is wearing

- Children MUST get permission to put their finger/knee/elbow on the item of clothing that has the colour mentioned

10. ENDING RITUAL

Pass a back rub. Remind children that they have a right to sit out rather than feel they have to participate.

11. ASSESSMENT

Children can talk about what makes them feel OK and what makes them feel not OK.

12. RESOURCES

- Its My Body by Lory Freeman, ISBN 0-943990-03-3, obtainable from Smallwood Publishing

  Tel: 01304 2269900

- Music

- Puppet

Learn to keep themselves and others safe

Foundation Lesson 6

I am going to learn about safe and unsafe secrets

Prior to this Quality Circle Time read *The Trouble with Secrets, K. Johnson, ISBN0943990226*, obtainable from Smallwood Publishing, Tel: 01304 2269900.

The story helps children distinguish between worrying secrets and surprises. It also presents many different 'secrets' for children to consider.

You may choose to use the following scenarios prior to Quality Circle Time:

1.Tell the children that you intend giving one of the school staff a gift, perhaps for their contribution to the school

Show the children the gift • Ask them to keep it a secret • Discuss whether this secret is an OK secret

2. Puppet tells the children that he has broken his friends toy

He says that he is going to pretend that he knows nothing about it • Will the children keep his secret? • Discuss whether this secret is an OK secret • What makes it not OK?

1. THE MAIN AREA OF STUDY SUGGESTS THAT PUPILS SHOULD:	2. KEY LEARNING OBJECTIVES
SKILLS ● Able to differentiate between safe or an unsafe secret	● I can tell the difference between safe and unsafe secrets
ATTITUDES ● Care about keeping themselves and others safe	● I care about myself and other people
KNOWLEDGE/UNDERSTANDING ● Know what trust means	● I know what trust means

3. GROUND RULES	4. SKILLS AWARENESS
● We listen to each other ● We do not say or do anything that would hurt another person ● We signal when we want to say something	● Concentrating ● Listening ● Looking ● Speaking ● Thinking Throughout Quality Circle Time it is vital that practitioners praise children for using the above skills

5. GAME 1

The children dance around to the music

When the music stops the practitioner calls 'Hedgehogs'

- All the children drop to the floor, curl up in a ball and close their eyes
- The practitioner covers one child with a blanket. Remember to ask the child for permission before doing this. The children have to guess who is hidden. They can ask the hidden child to count, sing a song or answer simple questions to help.

6. ROUND 1

Ask children who they could tell if someone told them a not OK secret.

Trigger sentence:

I could tell...

Remind the children:

- Tell a secret if it makes you feel upset
- Tell a secret if it frightens you
- Tell a secret if you feel worried

7. SILENT STATEMENTS

Stand up and cross the circle if:

Your coat has a zip in it

Your shoes have laces

You think you should tell if your friend asks you to keep a secret about playing with matches

You think you should tell if your friend tells you what he has bought for his daddy's birthday

You think you should tell it someone touches you in a way you don't like

8. OPEN FORUM

Puppet has got a secret and he doesn't know whether to share it or not. The practitioner asks the children if they will help puppet to decide whether he should tell or not.

The practitioner asks the children to tell puppet when you should tell a secret.

Refer to round 1

Children respond

Eventually puppet tells the children that one of the other puppets has been hurting him. The other puppet has told puppet that he must keep it a secret or he'll hurt him some more. What should puppet do?

Children respond

9. GAME 2

Read out different 'secret' statements. Ask children to move either to the right, to the left or to the middle of the circle depending on their response.

Identify left, right and middle with colour labels.

To the right of the circle- I would tell

To the left of the circle- I would not tell

To the middle –I'm not sure

- Dad shows you a special birthday present for mum
- Some children have broken a window and tell you not to tell
- Someone is hurting you
- Someone has made a special cake for your practitioner's birthday

For children who, developmentally, are not at this level of response we suggest you ask them to call out 'tell' or 'don't tell' in response to the scenario

10. ENDING RITUAL

Whispers

The practitioner passes a secret word around the circle

Does the word remain the same?

Do include community language words

11. ASSESSMENT

Children can talk about a safe and unsafe secret

You could use Game 2 as part of your observation for this assessment

12. RESOURCES

- Activity 5 – Tell, Don't Tell Symbols

- Puppet

- Blanket

Learn to keep themselves and others safe

Foundation Lesson 7

As this lesson is a celebration of achievement you could in the week prior to the session involve children in planning the celebration event. You could:

- Get the children to send invitations to parents, governors as part of their literacy work
- Prepare celebration food lists
- Go shopping for food
- Prepare food
- Vote on favourite games to be played during the Quality Circle Time

1. THE MAIN AREA OF STUDY SUGGESTS THAT PUPILS SHOULD:	2. KEY LEARNING OBJECTIVES
SKILLS • Express and communicate their ideas, thoughts and feelings	• I am beginning to talk about my feelings
ATTITUDES • Appreciate the need to take care and for safe actions	• I am beginning to take care of myself
KNOWLEDGE/UNDERSTANDING • Think about themselves and their experiences	• I know what a safe action means • I can look back and begin to talk about the things that I have learned

3. GROUND RULES	4. SKILLS AWARENESS
• We listen to each other • We do not say or do anything that would hurt another person • We signal when we want to say something	• Concentrating • Listening • Looking • Speaking • Thinking Throughout Quality Circle Time it is vital that practitioners praise children for using the above skills

5. GAME 1	6. ROUND 1
Prior to this Quality Circle Time, make a list of the different games children have been introduced to. Ask them to vote for their favourite game. (You could: Ask the children to place their name card in the box with a label/picture of their favourite game. Alternatively, you could use a tally chart with labels/pictures for children to tick their favourite game)	Look back and remind children of the different experiences they have encountered. Use all the puppets you have introduced to the children to help you do this. e.g. **Puppet 1:** I remember when we looked in the plastic mirror and said how we were feeling. I liked that. **Puppet 2:** I remember when the puppet in lesson 2 hadn't got any friends. I felt really sorry for Puppet. The practitioner reminds children of the importance of 'listening' to their feelings. Explain that feelings help us to: ● Understand why we do things ● Understand why other people do things ● Know if something is OK or not OK **Trigger sentence:** Today I am feeling (pass the mirror that you used in lesson one)

7. SILENT STATEMENTS	8. OPEN FORUM
Stand up and cross the circle if: You have a sister You have a baby at home You feel happy today You know what you would do if you were lost You know what to do if someone is hitting you You think we are all special	For this session Open Forum is omitted. It is important that children have an opportunity to reflect on their learning and their achievements. You could invite parents and your visitor from focussed activity, page 11, to present certificates to the children. We have provided a partially completed certificate that could be used with the children to complete with the assistance of the practitioner. We suggest that you set up the circle using items that will enhance the specialness of the occasion, e.g. Flowers, candles, music

9. GAME 2	10. ENDING RITUAL
Favourite chosen game 2	The practitioner reminds the children about how special everyone is. The children end the Quality Circle Time by: Standing up and holding hands in the circle Next they swing their arms as they chant 'We are special' On the word special they all, still holding hands raise their arms above their heads. Then they lower their arms and repeat the sentence.

11. ASSESSMENT	12. RESOURCES
From the assessment evidence you have collected whilst working on this unit, we suggest you make a brief summative assessment of children's learning to include in a child's profile.	● All puppets from previous sessions ● Candles ● Activity Sheet 6 - Certificate ● Flowers ● Special food

Medium Term Planning Unit 2

Focus of Interest
KEEPING MYSELF SAFE (SUBSTANCES)

Expected Duration
(to be completed by practitioner)

FOCUS
Keeping Myself Safe (Substances)
KEY AREAS OF LEARNING : Personal, Social and Emotional Development, Physical Development Communication, Language and Literacy

Children will have opportunities to learn:

SKILLS

Knowing whom to go to for help and how to ask for help

Following simple safety rules and instructions

Apply practices for keeping safe

Expressing feelings such as concerns about illness and taking medicines

ATTITUDES

Develop respect for self and others

Value themselves and others

Appreciate the need to take care and for safe actions

Care about keeping themselves and others safe

KNOWLEDGE & CONCEPTS

Know that all substances can be harmful if not used property

Know and understand simple safety rules about medicines, tablets, solvents, and household substances

Know what is safe to put into/onto the body

Know rules for, and ways of, keeping safe

Know which people are involved with medicines (such as health professionals, shopkeepers)

Know about the dangers from handling discarded syringes and needles

Know people who can help them to stay safe

FOCUSED ACTIVITIES AND EXPERIENCES:	Early Learning Goals
Visits to a clinic, chemists, Health Centre.	PhD5
Invite a health professional (nurse, doctor, health visitor, chemist) into setting. Prepare children to listen and ask questions.	PhD5
Invite an aromatherapist to visit setting.	PhD5
Send thank-you notes to visitors.	CLL8
Set up a health related role play area (choose from those places visited).	CLL2/CLL3
Take on roles in health related role-play area (one of above), with adult support.	CLL7
Introduce scenarios into role-play for children to problem solve. E.g. some tablets have gone missing at the beginning of a session. What should we do?	CLL8/PSE8
Set up scenario of a baby needing a vaccination. Send postcard from clinic. Talk with children about their experiences of vaccinations/injections and safety regarding needles.	CLL3/CLL14 PSE3
Children make and write 'Get Well' cards to characters (perhaps one of the puppets) who are unwell/poorly. Talk about their experiences of being unwell.	CLL18/PSE4
Children write/make warning labels for home corner.	
Support the interactive display of safe/unsafe things to put into and on to our bodies.	CLL19 PhD5

ENHANCEMENTS OF BASIC PROVISION AND INTERACTIVE DISPLAYS

Small world – emergency vehicles and road map with hospital on

Small construction – Duplo Lego hospital set

Writing area – get well cards as examples, word banks of associated words

Home corner – introduce a medicine cabinet

Interactive display – sort safe/unsafe items to put on/into our bodies

INVOLVEMENT OF PARENTS

Newsletter home informing about theme and asking parents to reinforce safety rules about medicines.

Invite parents in to see, hear and experience the aromatherapist or other visitors.

RESOURCES: EQUIPMENT, MATERIALS, PICTURES

Pictures and labels of health professionals

Resource box for health related role play

Uniforms and equipment for health professionals

RESOURCES: BOOKS, POEMS, SONGS, RHYMES

Miss Polly had a Dolly

VOCABULARY

Poorly, unwell, fit, healthy, well,

Doctor, nurse, health visitor, chemist, thermometer,

Medicine, tablets, pills, prescription, injection,

Safe/unsafe, danger

QUESTIONS (PRESENT, FUTURE, PAST)

Can you tell me about a time when you have visited the doctor, hospital, etc?

How did you feel when you were poorly?

What made you feel better when?

What do you think Teddy needs to make him feel better?

What would you do if …

OBSERVATIONAL ASSESSMENT OPPORTUNITIES

At interactive display table observe and talk with children about safe and unsafe items.

(Please refer to assessment section included in lesson plans).

Evaluation

What went well?

What would I change next time?

Feedback from Children

Feedback from parents

Learn to keep themselves and others safe

Foundation Lesson 1

I am going to learn about what goes onto my body

1. THE MAIN AREA OF STUDY SUGGESTS THAT PUPILS SHOULD:	2. KEY LEARNING OBJECTIVES
SKILLS ● Apply practices for keeping safe	● I am beginning to show that I can think of different ways to keep myself safe ● I try to think before I act
ATTITUDES ● Appreciate the need to take care and for safe actions ● Care about keeping themselves and others safe	● I show, through my actions, that I care about my safety and my peer groups safety
KNOWLEDGE/UNDERSTANDING ● Know what is safe to put into/onto the body	● I can tell you what is safe and what is not safe to put onto my body

3. GROUND RULES	4. SKILLS AWARENESS
● We listen to each other ● We do not say or do anything that would hurt another person ● We signal when we want to say something	● Concentrating ● Listening ● Looking ● Speaking ● Thinking Throughout Quality Circle Time it is vital that practitioners praise children for using the above skills

5. GAME 1

- Gather together a range of different objects that are put onto the body, e.g. sun cream, sunglasses, hairbrush, prescribed ointment, bleach, cat flea powder
- The practitioner says:

  I went into the garden and put -------- onto my body

  I went into the bathroom and put --------- onto my body
- Children go to the right if they think that is OK, to the left if they think that it's not OK and the middle if they are not sure
- Identify right, left and middle with colour labels or faces

For children who, developmentally, are not at this level of response we suggest you ask them to call out 'it's O.K or it's not O.K'

6. ROUND 1

Ask children to reflect on all the things that have gone onto their bodies from the time they have got up

Trigger sentence:

I've put -------- onto my body

Discuss with the children the different feelings they have when things go onto their bodies. Look at the objects and pictures and ask children to say which things feel good and which things feel not so good. Ask children to consider which of the objects might be dangerous. Can they say why?

7. SILENT STATEMENTS

Stand up and cross the circle if:

You've got a plaster on your body

You've got glasses on

You've used a toothbrush today

A bee or wasp has stung your body

You can think of something not safe to put onto your body

8. OPEN FORUM

Puppet isn't anywhere to be seen. Your children might like to call for puppet. The practitioner eventually finds puppet hiding and looking very scared. Puppet is hiding his hand.

Practitioner
Puppet where have you been?

Puppet
[No response]

Practitioner
Puppet you look very scared. We can only help you if you talk to us.

Practitioner
Children can you think of how we might get puppet to talk to us. Encourage the children to reflect on how they feel when they are scared and frightened. What helps/hinders?

Children respond
Eventually puppet tells the class that he and some other puppets were playing with an unknown substance, e.g. a strange liquid. Puppet got some of the liquid on his hand. It is making his hand sting.

Practitioner
Go through with the children what puppet should do. Ask the children to compile some safety rules for puppet (you could display these in the area and also send them home for parents to display at home).

9. GAME 2	10. ENDING RITUAL
The practitioner plays the traditional game of Simon Says with the following adaptation: When Simon tells the children to put something unsafe onto their bodies the children shout 'Oh no, Simon!' When Simon tells them to put something safe onto their bodies they mime putting it on.	The practitioner begins by smiling at the child on the left of her. When the child on the left has been smiled at they repeat by smiling at the child on their left.

11. ASSESSMENT	12. RESOURCES
Children are able to sort objects into those that are safe to put onto their bodies and those that are not safe to put onto their bodies.	<ul><li>Objects that are put onto the body</li><li>Puppet</li></ul>

Learn to keep themselves and others safe

Foundation Lesson 2

I am going to learn about what goes into my body

1. THE MAIN AREA OF STUDY SUGGESTS THAT PUPILS SHOULD:	2. KEY LEARNING OBJECTIVES
SKILLS ● Apply practices for keeping safe **ATTITUDES** ● Appreciate the need to take care and for safe actions ● Care about keeping themselves and others safe **KNOWLEDGE/UNDERSTANDING** ● Know what is safe to put into the body	● I am beginning to show that I can think of different ways to keep myself safe ● I try to think before I act ● I show, through my actions, that I care about my safety and my peer groups safety ● I can tell you what is safe and what is not safe to put into my body

3. GROUND RULES	4. SKILLS AWARENESS
● We listen to each other ● We do not say or do anything that would hurt another person ● We signal when we want to say something	● Concentrating ● Listening ● Looking ● Speaking ● Thinking Throughout Quality Circle Time it is vital that practitioners praise children for using the above skills

5. GAME 1

- The practitioner reminds the children of the previous lesson.

- What can the children remember?

- What skill is particularly important in keeping safe.

- The practitioner reminds the children that learning how to listen is extremely important. She tells the children that they are going to play a game that will help them to listen really carefully.

- The practitioner has three 'noises' hidden in a box e.g. a rattle, a whistle, a bell. Each noise has a different instruction, for example:

- Rattle: stand and wave to your friend

- Whistle: kneel on all fours

- Bell: jump up and down

- The children are to do the appropriate action when they hear the sound

6. ROUND 1

Ask children to reflect on all the things that have gone into their bodies from the time they have got up.

Trigger sentence:

I've put -------- into my body.

7. SILENT STATEMENTS

Stand up and cross the circle if:

You've put a cup of tea into your body this morning

You've had an injection put into your body

You've had a splinter in your body

You feel happy when you put ice-cream into your body

8. OPEN FORUM

Puppet is really excited. He's found a big bag of sweeties in the playground. 'Let's share them out' Puppet says

The practitioner asks the children what they might say to puppet

Children respond

You could follow this up by getting the children to come up with some basic safety rules

Use the safety rules in lesson 1 to discuss and reinforce key safety messages

9. GAME 2	10. ENDING RITUAL
The practitioner plays the traditional game of Simon Says with the following adaptation: When Simon tells the children to put something unsafe into their bodies the children shout 'Oh no, Simon!' When Simon tells them to put something safe into their bodies they mime putting it in.	The practitioner begins by smiling at the child on the left of her. When the child on the left has been smiled at they repeat by smiling at the child on their left.

11. ASSESSMENT	12. RESOURCES
Children are able to sort objects into those that are safe to put into their bodies and those that are not safe to put into their bodies.	<ul><li>Bell</li><li>Box</li><li>Brown paper bag with 'sweeties' inside</li><li>Objects that are put into the body</li><li>Puppet</li><li>Rattle</li><li>Whistle</li></ul>

Learn to keep themselves and others safe

Foundation Lesson 3

I am going to learn how I feel when I am ill

1. THE MAIN AREA OF STUDY SUGGESTS THAT PUPILS SHOULD:	2. KEY LEARNING OBJECTIVES
SKILLS ● Knowing whom to go for help and how to ask for help	● I can tell you what I feel like when I don't feel well
ATTITUDES ● Develop respect for self and others ● Value themselves and others	● I show that I care about myself and others
KNOWLEDGE/UNDERSTANDING ● Know that all substances can be harmful if not used properly ● Know and understand simple safety rules about medicines, tablets, solvents, and household substances	● I know that medicines can help me feel better but I also know that there are other ways of feeling better

3. GROUND RULES	4. SKILLS AWARENESS
● We listen to each other ● We do not say or do anything that would hurt another person ● We signal when we want to say something	● Concentrating ● Listening ● Looking ● Speaking ● Thinking Throughout Quality Circle Time it is vital that practitioners praise children for using the above skills

5. GAME 1

Sing with the children 'Miss Polly had a dolly'. Add miming actions to the song.

6. ROUND 1

Discuss with the children what they feel like when they are poorly.

- What might they say?
- What might they think/feel?
- What might they do?
- What might they want?

Trigger sentence:

When I am poorly I ...

7. SILENT STATEMENTS

Stand up and cross the circle if:

You feel poorly today

Someone in your house is poorly

You like being in bed when you're poorly

You don't like missing school/nursery when you are poorly

You like cuddles when you are poorly

You like to be left alone when you are poorly

8. OPEN FORUM

The practitioner tells the children that Teddy is poorly. She's not sure what the matter is because Teddy doesn't want to say anything.

How can we help Teddy?

The practitioner uses the following key questions to help the children decide on the best action for Teddy.

How does Teddy look?

What is Teddy doing / not doing?

What is Teddy asking for?

What might help Teddy to get better?

[Help children to realise that medicine may be necessary, but not always]

9. GAME 2	10. ENDING RITUAL
Sing with the children 'Miss Polly had a dolly'. Add miming actions to the song.	The children shake hands with the partner on their left saying, 'Thank you for Quality Circle Time'.

11. ASSESSMENT	12. RESOURCES
Ask the children if they can tell you what Teddy feels like when he is not well. Can the children suggest ways to help Teddy feel better?	● Activity Sheet 7 - Miss Polly had a Dolly ● Teddy

Learn to keep themselves and others safe

Foundation Lesson 4

I am going to learn about who needs medicines and I am going to learn about the safety rules to do with medicine

1. THE MAIN AREA OF STUDY SUGGESTS THAT PUPILS SHOULD:	2. KEY LEARNING OBJECTIVES
SKILLS ● Following simple safety rules and instructions	● I show through my actions that I can follow simple safety rules and instructions
ATTITUDES ● Value themselves and others	● I show through my words and actions that I value myself and others
KNOWLEDGE/UNDERSTANDING ● Know and understand simple safety rules about medicines, tablets, solvents, and household substances ● Know which people are involved with medicines (such as health professionals, shopkeepers)	● I can tell you the rules about medicines

3. GROUND RULES	4. SKILLS AWARENESS
● We listen to each other ● We do not say or do anything that would hurt another person ● We signal when we want to say something	● Concentrating ● Listening ● Looking ● Speaking ● Thinking Throughout Quality Circle Time it is vital that practitioners praise children for using the above skills

5. GAME 1

The practitioner places six mats around the circle. In front of each mat is a sign and a picture:

- Sweetshop
- Doctor's Surgery
- Chemist
- Dentist
- Supermarket
- Post Office

The practitioner plays music and the children move around 'visiting' each area as they go.

When the music stops the practitioner calls out:

'Where will we go today?'

The children respond:

'Tell us what we're going for?'

The practitioner says:

You're going to see someone about your poorly tummy

The children visit the appropriate area

6. ROUND 1

The practitioner asks the children about their experiences to do with medicines.

Who needs medicines?

Who told the children to take the medicine?

Was the person a safe person?

Who gave the medicine to them?

Trigger Statement:

I had some medicine when…

7. SILENT STATEMENTS

Stand up and cross the circle if:

You use a spray for when you wheeze

You've had some medicine for a cough

You've been in hospital

You feel sad/lonely/cared when you're poorly

You feel sad/lonely scared if someone in your family is poorly

You have visited someone in hospital

You can think of a nice thing to say/do when someone is poorly

8. OPEN FORUM

Puppet has been to the doctor. The practitioner asks the children if they would like to ask puppet any questions.

If the children do not ask about medicines the practitioner tells the children that puppet has some medicine.

Make sure you cover the following safety rules in dialogue with the children and the puppet.

- Who gave puppet the medicine?
- Where should the medicine be stored?
- How do we know that the medicine is for puppet?

Safety rules

- All medicines have drugs in them
- You must only take medicines from a safe person
- You must never take anyone
- You must never take anyone else's medicine
- If someone tries to persuade you to take or touch something practise saying 'No, I won't' or 'I'll ask …' or 'I'll tell someone'

9. GAME 2

Place 6 pictures of people doing different jobs around the room

- A police person
- A doctor/nurse
- A shop keeper
- A teacher
- A crossing patrol person
- A post person

The practitioner plays music and the children move around 'visiting' each person as they go. When the music stops the practitioner calls out:

'Who should we see today?'

The children respond:

'Tell us what we're going to see them for.'

The practitioner says:

'You need to see some one about your poorly toe.'

The children respond:

'We need to see…'

The children visit the appropriate area

10. ENDING RITUAL

Children pass a back rub around the circle

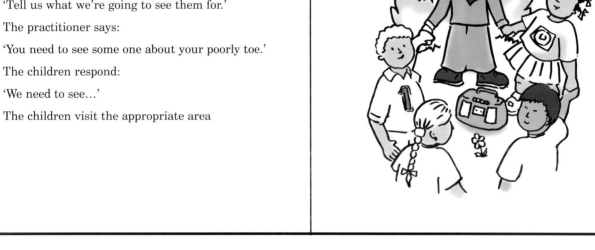

11. ASSESSMENT

Children can tell or draw simple safety rules. They are beginning to explain why such rules are necessary.

12. RESOURCES

- Puppet
- Activity Sheet 8 - Safety Rules
- Activity Sheet 9 - Place Mat Game
- Activity Sheet 10 - People Who Help

Learn to keep themselves and others safe

Foundation Lesson 5

I am going to learn about who can help me stay safe

1. THE MAIN AREA OF STUDY SUGGESTS THAT PUPILS SHOULD:	2. KEY LEARNING OBJECTIVES
SKILLS ● Knowing whom to go for help and how to ask for help	● I can ask for help
ATTITUDES ● Value themselves and others ● Appreciate the need to take care ● Care about keeping themselves and others safe	● I show that I care about myself and others through the safe actions I take
KNOWLEDGE/UNDERSTANDING ● Know about the dangers from handling discarded syringes and needles	● I know why I mustn't touch syringes, broken glass, etc.

3. GROUND RULES	4. SKILLS AWARENESS
● We listen to each other ● We do not say or do anything that would hurt another person ● We signal when we want to say something	● Concentrating ● Listening ● Looking ● Speaking ● Thinking Throughout Quality Circle Time it is vital that practitioners praise children for using the above skills

5. GAME 1

- Remind the children about the focus of the lesson. Teach them the poem I'm a little teapot.

- I'm a little teapot, short and stout,

  Here's my handle,

  Here's my spout,

  When I get the steam up, hear me shout,

  'Tip me up and pour me out'.

- Very briefly remind the children of the dangers of playing with hot liquids.

6. ROUND 1

Discuss with the children the basic rules of safety. Choose from the following rounds depending on the children's confidence.

- I can stay safe by… or
- I mustn't touch…

7. SILENT STATEMENTS

Stand up and cross the circle if:

You're wearing red

You've helped a friend today

You get scared if someone tries to make you do something you don't want to do

You can say, 'No, I don't want to do that…'

You can tell me a safety rule

8. OPEN FORUM

Teddy is very quiet.

I wonder why Teddy is quiet the practitioner asks.

The children respond.

Teddy begins to tell the children about what happened the previous day at the park. Teddy and his friend were playing near the swings. They saw something near the swings something Teddy shouldn't touch.

Ask the children if they can guess what it was.

The children respond.

Teddy shows the children a picture of a syringe. Teddy's daddy was very cross because Teddy and his friend had picked up the syringe and begun playing with it.

'Why shouldn't I have played with it' Teddy asks the children

The children respond.

The practitioner talks to the children about picking up discarded syringes. The children tell Teddy some of the things that are safe to play with and some of the things, which aren't.

9. GAME 2

- Teach the children the words to Doggy on the railway. You can add your own words, sounds and actions to make the poem come alive!

Doggy on the railway,

Shouldn't be there,

Along came an engine,

Doggy take care!

'Hey!' said the driver,

'Get off the track.'

Doggy ran away then,

And NEVER CAME BACK!

10. ENDING RITUAL

Children pass a handshake around the circle saying, 'Stay safe...'.

11. ASSESSMENT

Give the children photographs of things that are safe to play with and things that are not. Can the children sort the photographs into safe and not safe sets?

Are the children comfortable with asking for help?

12. RESOURCES

- Activity Sheet 11 - Syringe
- Teddy

Learn to keep themselves and others safe

Foundation Lesson 6

As this lesson is a celebration of achievement you could in the week prior to the session involve children in planning the celebration event. You could:

- Get the children to send invitations to parents, governors as part of their literacy work
- Prepare celebration food lists
- Go shopping for food
- Prepare food
- Vote on favourite games to be played during the Quality Circle Time

1. THE MAIN AREA OF STUDY SUGGESTS THAT PUPILS SHOULD:	2. KEY LEARNING OBJECTIVES
SKILLS • Follow simple safety rules and instructions	• I know some simple safety rules
ATTITUDES • Appreciate the need to care about keeping themselves and others safe	• I am beginning to take care of myself and others
KNOWLEDGE/UNDERSTANDING • Know that all substances can be harmful if not used properly	• know that all substances can be harmful if they are not used properly • I can look back and talk about the things I have learned

3. GROUND RULES	4. SKILLS AWARENESS
• We listen to each other • We do not say or do anything that would hurt another person • We signal when we want to say something	• Concentrating • Listening • Looking • Speaking • Thinking Throughout Quality Circle Time it is vital that practitioners praise children for using the above skills

5. GAME 1

Prior to this Quality Circle Time, make a list of the different games children have been introduced to. Ask them to vote for their favourite game.

(You could: Ask the children to place their name card in the box with a label/picture of their favourite game. Alternatively, you could use a tally chart with labels/pictures for children tick their favourite game)

6. ROUND 1

Look back and remind children of the different experiences they have encountered. Use all the puppets you have introduced to the children to help you do this.

e.g. **Puppet 1** says 'I remember when I put some thing on my hand…it was really stinging. Thank you children, you helped me to do the right thing.'

e.g. **Puppet 2** says 'I remember finding a bag of sweeties. The children really helped me to learn what to do'.

After recapping on the different sessions ask the children to say what they have learned.

Trigger statement:

I've learned that…

7. SILENT STATEMENTS

Stand up and cross the circle if:

You're wearing something blue

You're wearing trousers

You feel well/not well today

You're feeling tired/not tired today

You can tell me a safety rule

You know what to do if you saw a syringe in the playground

8. OPEN FORUM

For this session Open Forum is omitted. It is important that children have an opportunity to reflect on their learning and their achievements. We have provided a partially completed certificate that could be used with the children to complete with assistance of the practitioner. You could invite parents and a chosen visitor to present certificates to the children. We suggest that you set up the circle using items that will enhance the specialness of the occasion e.g. Flowers, candles, music

Use the puppets to say thank you to the children for helping them with their learning.

9. GAME 2	10. ENDING RITUAL
Favourite chosen game 2	The practitioner reminds the children about how special everyone is. The children end the Quality Circle Time by: Standing up and holding hands in the circle Next they swing their arms as they chant 'We are special' On the word special they all, still holding hands raise their arms above their heads. Then they lower their arms and repeat the sentence.

11. ASSESSMENT	12. RESOURCES
From the assessment evidence you have collected whilst working on this unit, we suggest you make a brief summative assessment of children's learning to include in a child's profile	• All puppets from previous sessions • Candles • Activity Sheet 6 • Flowers • Music • Special food

Resource Bank

Activity Sheet 1

Feeling Faces

HAPPY

SAD

ANGRY

MAD

Activity Sheet 1

Feeling Faces

LONELY

EXCITED

SCARED

FRIGHTENED

Activity Sheet 2

Animal Picture Cards

Activity Sheet 3

Scared Heart

Activity Sheet 4

Letter from Grandad

Dear Mrs Begum

I hope you can help me.

Yesterday Leo was playing in the garden. When I came to tell him that his dinner was ready he wasn't there. He had gone!

I went running up the street calling his name and he came round the corner with some big children. They told me they had taken Leo to play football on the field because he looked lonely on his own.

I have talked to Leo about this. Please Mrs Begum can you and the children talk to Leo as well and help him understand what he must do to keep safe.

Thank you Mrs Begum.

Grandad

Begum

ly Bush Road

LS1 2AB

Activity Sheet 5

Tell or Don't Tell Symbols

I would tell

I would not tell

I am not sure

Activity Sheet 6

Certificate

WELL DONE!

In our class we have been learning how to keep safe

I have learned how to...

Miss Polly Had a Dolly

Miss Polly had a dolly
who was sick, sick sick.
So she phoned for the doctor
to be quick, quick, quick.
the doctor came
with his bag and his hat,
And he knocked at the door
with a rat, a tat, tat.

He looked at the dolly
and he shook his head
And he said Miss Polly
put her straight to bed.
He wrote on a paper
for a pill, pill, pill.
I'll be back in the morning,
with my bill, bill, bill.

Activity Sheet 8

Safety Rules

All medicines have drugs in them

•

You must only take medicines from a safe person

•

You must never take anyone else's medicine

•

If someone tries to persuade you to take or touch something, practise saying ' No, I won't' or 'I'll ask' or 'I'll tell someone'.

Activity Sheet 9

Place Mat Game

Dentist

Doctors

Sweetshop

Supermarket

Chemist

Post Office

Activity Sheet 10

People who help

A doctor

A crossing patrol person

A shopkeeper

A police person

A teacher

A post person

Activity Sheet 11

Syringe

Further Reading

Useful Publications

- **It's my Body*** by Lory Freeman, ISBN 094399033 (Smallwood Publishing)

- **Poems for Circle Time and Literacy Hour** by Margaret Goldthorpe (LDA)

- **The Trouble with Secrets*** by K. Johnson, ISBN 0943990226(Smallwood Publishing)

- **Training Video: Quality Circle Time in Action** (LDA)

- **Photocopiable Materials for use with the Jenny Mosley Circle Time Model** by Jenny Mosley (Positive Press)

- **More Quality Circle Time** by Jenny Mosley (LDA)

- **Quality Circle Time in the Primary Classroom** by Jenny Mosley (LDA)

- **Here We Go Round** by Jenny Mosley and Helen Sonnet (Positive Press)

- **Stepping Stones To Success** by Helen Sonnet & Pat Child (Positive Press)

All above, except for those marked* are available from:

Positive Press Ltd 28a Gloucester Road, Trowbridge, Wiltshire BA14 0AA.

Tel: 01225 719204   Fax: 01225 712187

Email: circletime@jennymosley.demon.co.uk

Website: www.circle-time.co.uk